INHERITANCE

WHAT JESUS LEFT US AND WHAT THE ENEMY HAS TRIED TO STEAL

BRIAN PRUITT

INHERITANCE

Copyright © 2025 by PRUITT MOTIVATIONAL

Published BY: PRUITT MOTIVATIONAL BOOKS

www.Pruittmotivational.com

www.Powerofdad.org

INHERITANCE:

What Jesus left us and what the enemy has tried to steal

By: Brian Pruitt

Printed in the USA by 48 Hour Books (www.48HrBooks.com)

ISBN:

Book was designed and artwork done by: Chris Molitor

Contact Info: cbmolitor@gmail.com

**BOOKS THAT MOTIVATE
THE GIANT INSIDE!**

DEDICATION

To my wife and children: I pray that God reveals all we are meant to become and that we embrace it while we're still alive. You are my inheritance. My wife Delicia and my children Brianna, Destiny, Brian & Diamond, I love you. GBG - Go Be Great!

Table of Contents

WORD FROM THE AUTHOR:

This book is not about acquiring items but discovering your identity. Material things fade, but spiritual treasures endure forever. May each chapter bring fresh revelation that you embody and live out while on Earth. Inheritance!

Sincerely Yours

Brian Pruitt

All kings and queens are not born of royal bloodlines. Some become royal because of what they do once they realize who they are.

CHAPTER 1

SUDDENLY ROYAL

Suddenly Royal

Like a laser, the sun shot through the window blinds that David forgot to close tightly before he went to bed the night before. Each sunray danced across his face like a well-trained performer. Simultaneously, the screaming sound of his alarm clock pierced his ears. With hopes of getting a little more sleep, David rolled over, grabbed his flimsy pillow, and covered his head. Just then, he felt a familiar sharp pain; it was his wife Pam using her pointy elbow, nudging him in the back. "Make it stop!" She said this, referring to the alarm. David rolled back over, hit the off button on the alarm clock, and lay in bed for a minute thinking. I wish I could control several things in my life, like my alarm clock, and MAKE THEM STOP!

Like many of us, David and his wife's lives had become meager compared to their childhood dreams. Life had become a thief who sneaked in during the middle of the night and stole their dreams. David often said to himself, "There must be more!"

David and his wife, trapped in the mundane routine of life, had become a version of the Walking Dead. Each day was a repetition of the last until one day, everything changed. David, the auto repairman, was about to have a life-changing revelation.

One of David's hobbies was researching his family history. One day, David and his wife stumbled upon a surprising revelation. It just so happened that David was the last remaining relative of a king—yes, a king. David was a descendant of royal blood. He was a distant cousin of Queen Elizabeth II of England, but he also discovered he was a direct descendant of Thomas II, the last King of the Isle of Mann.

The repairman suddenly became royal. David had an actual claim to the title of King of the Isle of Mann. In March 2007, David was officially crowned king. The next ten years of his life would be very different.

What If?

What if David had only known he was a king from birth? I wonder how differently he would have lived his life. Would he have moved with a different level of confidence, authority, and boldness? Would he have dreamed a little bigger, made different decisions, and taken risks without fear?

The truth is, David was actually a king from birth; it just took him many years to discover it. Discovering his inheritance changed his life. In the same way, discovering your inheritance will change your life.

What if I told you that many of us, as children of God, live lives that resemble David's life in many ways? We, too, wake up struggling to face life because we don't know who we are. Are you living without joy because you don't know it's your inheritance? Are you living without peace and finding it hard to sleep at night because you don't know peace is your inheritance? King David in the Bible says it this way in Psalms 103:1-5 Bless the LORD, O my soul, And forget not all His benefits: Who forgives all your iniquities, Who heals all your diseases, Who redeems your life from destruction,

Who crowns you with lovingkindness and tender mercies, Who satisfies your mouth with good things, So that your youth is renewed like the eagle's.

Why was David saying bless the Lord, oh my soul? Because God had left him an inheritance. David even went as far as to name some things he had inherited as a child of God. David had inherited forgiveness, healing, safety, loving-kindness, mercy, and the renewal of his youth. He was excited that he had been left an inheritance. I wrote this book to remind us that you and I have also been given an inheritance. Like King David, we, too, should be demanding our souls to bless God for the inheritance we have been given.

Your inheritance is where you will find your benefits. If we don't understand the inheritance we have been left as believers, we can live mediocre lives when God has called us to be great and impact the world. We can live as citizens, all the while never knowing that we were born rulers, kings, and queens.

Your life was not meant to be mundane. **God has created you to (Carpe Diem) seize the day, not to be seized by the day.**

What if I told you something happened when Christ died on the cross? Something so powerful that all of heaven and hell stood at attention and took notice. Something so powerful that Satan gathered every demon in hell and gave them one assignment: steal our inheritance. Why? Because you and I have suddenly become royal. Christ's death changed everything. It took us from regular to royal. Jesus often spoke of the Kingdom of God. The question is, why? He was trying to get his royal subjects, you and I, to understand that we were kings and queens. He came to earth with a message. That message was the revelation of who we were in Him. Identity in Christ! Jesus came to tell us about our inheritance, hoping we would walk in it and dominate the earth. Jesus made us, Suddenly Royal! **Not all kings and queens are born of royal bloodlines. Some become royal because of what they do once they realize who they are.**

CHAPTER 2

DEFINING INHERITANCE

Defining Inheritance

You must have an understanding of something in order to walk in it. Otherwise, you will forfeit what you do not understand. For the most part, as children of God, this is precisely what has happened: **we have forfeited what we have failed to understand.**

God forbid we get to heaven and find rooms full of spiritual gifts, talents, healings, miracles, signs, and wonders, a victorious life all sitting unused and unlived, only to discover they all belonged to us. They are gifts, talents, healings, miracles, signs, and wonders, and a life that God wanted us to walk in, but we did not. They went unused, unwrapped, and unlived because we never walked in or understood our inheritance. So before we go any further, let's get an understanding.

Inheritance: The Latin root is inhereditare, which means "to appoint as heir." **This word literally means to go from second place to present and active. Simply put, it means To Become Something.**

Interestingly, the definition of the word inheritance changed in the 14th century. The meaning went from being appointed as something or somebody to simply receiving something, such as material things. When the meaning changed, society's response changed as well. Instead of stretching our hand out to be crowned the next king or queen, we stretched our hand out to see what material things we could possess after someone passed away. It was never meant to be this way. The getting should have taken place because of who we were becoming, not simply based on Webster's dictionary definition, which is: The acquisition of property. We acquire because of who we are, sons and daughters of God.

Somewhere in history, we, as children of God, started asking the wrong question; we should be asking who am I, not what can I get. We lost the revelation of who we were in Christ Jesus, and in doing so, we have become content with being ruled by things instead of being rulers of things. God made his plan for mankind clear in:

Genesis 1:28

And God blessed them, and God said unto them, Be fruitful, and multiply, and replenish the earth, and subdue it: **and have dominion over the fish of the sea, and over the fowl of the air, and over every living thing that moveth upon the earth.**

God goes deeper into this matter by stating what the result of us forfeiting our inheritance has brought about. Proverbs 23:7 says, For as a man thinketh in his heart, so is he…

Simply put, we thought less of ourselves. **We forfeited our inheritance, and we became less than what God created us to be. We settled for getting instead of becoming.**

God did not just want us to receive something. It was his heart's desire for us to BECOME or be something or somebody. God wanted us to BECOME INHERITORS, SECONDS that moved into FIRST. Seconds that moved into present active duty as kings and queens. God was saying that you are heirs. You are not me but you get to act and move as me.

Becoming vs. Receiving

Becoming is the trademark of a mature believer. While only receiving is the sign of an immature son or daughter. Throughout scripture, God makes the dividing line between the mature and the immature very clear. From the Old Testament all the way to the New Testament, God was trying to get his sons and daughters to BECOME.

The Israelites wanted to **receive** deliverance from Pharaoh, but God wanted them to **become** his people, his bride. The Hebrews failed to realize their forty-year journey through the wilderness was about becoming. It was about God showing himself to them in the midst of the journey. He wanted to show them through the plagues that he would move heaven and earth to rescue them so that they could become… He wanted to show them as a fire by day and a cloud by night that he would never leave them. He wanted to show them at the Red Sea as sons and daughters that all things were possible. He wanted to show them through giving them manna from heaven to eat so that they would not starve in the desert that He was their provider. Sadly, the Hebrews complained against God. They showed their immaturity by focusing on what they could receive instead of who they were becoming. They were so immature that God left them to wander in the desert for forty years. He left them to wander until the next generation grew up and asked, "Who are we?" "What have we become?" "Who did God create us to become?" It was that generation that entered into the promised land. The generation that was mature enough to focus on becoming, not just receiving.

In the book of Luke 15:11-32 is the story of a royal son who refused to become. This royal son only wanted to receive. We know him as the Prodigal Son.

Verses 11-14 says, "There was a man who had two sons. The younger one said to his father, 'Father, **GIVE ME** my share of the estate.' So he divided his property between them. "Not long after that, the younger son got together all he had, set off for a distant country and there squandered his wealth in wild living. After he had spent everything, there was a severe famine in that whole country, and he began to be in need.

Verses 15-22 goes on to say, So he went and hired himself out to a citizen of that country, who sent him to his fields to feed pigs. He longed to fill his stomach with the pods that the pigs were eating, but no one gave him anything. "When he came to his senses, he said, 'How many of my father's hired servants have food to spare, and here I am starving to death! I will set out and go back to my father and say to him: Father, I have sinned against heaven and against you.

I am no longer worthy to be called your son; make me like one of your hired servants. So he got up and went to his father. "But while he was still a long way off, his father saw him and was filled with compassion for him; he ran to his son, threw his arms around him and kissed him. "The son said to him, 'Father, I have sinned against heaven and against you. I am no longer worthy to be called your son. "But the father said to his servants, 'Quick! Bring the best robe and put it on him. Put a ring on his finger and sandals on his feet. Bring the fattened calf and kill it. Let's have a feast and celebrate. For this son of mine was dead and is alive again; he was lost and is found.' So they began to celebrate.

In other words this son of mine has moved from GIVE ME to who am I BECOMING. The father in this story was not just celebrating his son's return physically. He was celebrating his return mentally and spiritually. He celebrated his return to becoming. He celebrated the fact that his son had finally chosen to be mature and become.

When we mature, we move from "Give me! Give me! Give me! When we mature, we move to a mindset of, "Show me! Show me! Show me!" Show me who I am in you, Lord.

The final example I will give is that of the life of Judas, the betrayer. For thirty pieces of silver, he betrayed the King of Kings. He gave up a kingdom for a nickel. He gave up becoming for getting. When he realized that what he received could not measure up to what God wanted him to become, he took his life. We must learn to be content with becoming.

The Apostle Paul said it this way in Philippians 3:7-8 "But whatever were gains to me I now consider loss for the sake of Christ. What is more, I consider everything a loss because of the surpassing worth of knowing Christ Jesus my Lord, for whose sake I have lost all things. I consider them garbage, that I may gain Christ."

Paul was saying; I am content with becoming!

Inheritance Without Heredity

So, what's the problem? **The problem is that we often want inheritance without heredity.** We want stuff without sonship or daughtership. We want stuff without relationship and that just won't suffice for the victorious life that we were designed for. Why would we settle for junk when we can have the joy of the journey? Why be satisfied with water when you can have living water is what Jesus said to the woman at the well. Why be content with problems when you can have peace? Why dream of pits when God wants to put you in a palace? Why live in a cave when God has called you to inherit a kingdom?

Let me be very clear: there is no inheritance without heredity.

In other words, you must be part of the family or, at the very least, have been grafted/adopted into it.

Webster's Dictionary defines heredity as the transmission of qualities from ancestors to descendants through the genes. Heredity refers to traits and expressions that are passed on from one's parents.

This definition reminds me of Genesis 1:26, when God says, "Let us make man in our image." Since they will be sons and daughters, they must be made in our image. They must have our qualities, characteristics, and expressions. Why? Because they are family!

God speaks of our adoption process in Ephesians 1:4-5 **In love,** God predestined us for **adoption** to **sonship** through Jesus Christ, in accordance with his pleasure and will.

What a powerful passage of scripture. God says that our adoption process was motivated by love. He did not have to choose us, but he did. **We have been adopted and placed in the Will and Trust of our Father in heaven.**

The Bible is a story of adoption. 1 John 4:10 says, "This is love: not that we loved God, but that he loved us and sent his Son as an atoning sacrifice for our sins." This could also be read as follows:

"This is the adoption process, not that we chose God, but that God chose us and sent his Son as an atoning sacrifice for our sins."

Love saved the day. Love made a way. Love paid the price. Love made sure that your name was written in the Will. Love ensured that you and I had an inheritance in the kingdom of God.

CHAPTER 3

YOUR INHERITANCE
&
YOUR REDEEMER

The Kinsman Redeemer

God knew that there would be no inheritance without heredity, so he made us and called us his own. The Bible refers to this as a Kinsman Redeemer.

What is a Kinsman Redeemer? It is the Hebrew word Goel, from the root meaning to redeem. The Goel among the Hebrews was the nearest male blood <u>relation</u> <u>alive</u>. The Kinsman Redeemer or the Goel had important responsibilities placed upon him toward his next of kin and the next generation. They consisted of the following:

Promised Land

Land: If anyone was in poverty and was unable to redeem his inheritance, it was the duty of the kinsman to redeem it (Leviticus 25:25, Ruth 3:12)

For the Hebrews, it was God who gave the Land (Promised Land). He gave it to their forefathers, Abraham, Isaac, and Jacob, and it has been part of their inheritance ever since. He raised up Moses and Joshua to lead them into that land as Kinsmen Redeemers.

For us, the Promised Land is a Promised Kingdom—a kingdom that we get to walk in now and live in later. It is part of our inheritance. It is called the Kingdom of God. Jesus frequently referred to it by saying, "The kingdom of God is near." Another way of saying it would be: Your inheritance is here; now, walk in it. It has value now on earth and in the afterlife.

Freedom From Bondage

Bondage: He was also required to redeem his relatives who had been sold or taken into slavery (Leviticus 25:48, Leviticus 25:49). For the Hebrews, who at the time had been in bondage to the Egyptians for four hundred years, freedom was their heart's cry. It would take an inheritance to set them free.

The Kinsman Redeemer sent ten plagues. Ten plagues

that led to the freedom of God's people. We who may be fighting areas and issues in our lives that have tried to keep us in bondage can be sure of one thing: God will move heaven and earth to see us set free. **There is no beauty in being bound**. God, the Kinsman redeemer, wants us free. There is beauty in freedom. **God will send plagues against the very thing that has been a plague to you, and like the Israelites, you will be free**. It is part of your inheritance. Why? Because He loves you and desires you to have your inheritance.

The Avenger & Protector

Avenger: The Goel also was the avenger of blood if there was a murder of the next of kin. (Numbers 35:21) Vengeance is mine, says the Lord. God's protection is part of our inheritance. While this does not always mean that God will deal with your enemies the way you think they should be dealt with. What it does mean is that he will deal with them the way that he sees fit. The point of this scripture is to remind us that God is our defender and our avenger. That his defense is part of our inheritance.

As I write this book, Israel is at war with a militant nationalist group known as Hamas. They have killed and taken hostages from Palestinian people as well as Israel's people to further their cause. Their selfish ambition has hurt people on both sides. Since 2011, the skies over Isreal have been protected from attacks of war by what they call the Iron Dome. The Iron Dome is an Israeli mobile all-weather air defense system. The system is designed to intercept and destroy short-range rockets and artillery shells fired from distances up to forty-five miles away. Stopping any trajectory that would take them to an Israeli-populated area.

According to Psalms 125:1-2, we too have an Iron Dome; his name is Jesus. Psalms 125:1-2 says, "Those who trust in the Lord are like Mount Zion, which cannot be shaken but endures forever. As the mountains surround Jerusalem, so the Lord surrounds his people both now and forevermore."

God is our Iron Dome. This is part of our inheritance as sons and daughters of God. This is why God tells us in Isaiah 54:17 that **NO WEAPON** formed against us shall proposer.

Why? Because God is our Iron Dome! He is our avenger and our Kinsman Redeemer.

Chosen Heirs

Heir: Strange as this may sound, it served a purpose. The Kinsman Redeemer was required to marry his brother's widow if he were to die. The purpose was to ensure she had a child who could carry on the family name and receive an inheritance. While I am certainly not asking you to go to this extreme, there is a powerful truth to be pointed out here.

The Kinsman Redeemer was required to marry his brother's widow if he was to die. The purpose would be to make sure that she had a child who could carry on the family name and receive an inheritance. Let me remind you that we are the bride of Christ.

Isaiah 54:5 For your Maker is your husband, the Lord of hosts is his name; and the Holy One of Israel is your Redeemer, the God of the whole earth he is called.

We see this process put in place in my favorite scripture found in Psalms 68:5-6. A father to the fatherless, a defender of widows, is God in his holy dwelling. God sets the lonely in families, He leads out the prisoners with singing; but the rebellious live in a sun-scorched land.

God refuses to allow us to be fatherless or widowed. He is married to us. He refuses to allow us to lose our inheritance. He is committed to us becoming. The Kinsman Redeemer is committed to his heirs.

I have good news for you. Jesus is our Kinsman Redeemer, our Goel. (Exodus 6:6 ; Isaiah 43:1, 41:14, Isaiah 44:6 Isaiah 44:22, 48:20, Psalms 103:4)

CHAPTER 4

INHERITANCE vs. LEGACY

The Process

An inheritance is what you leave with people. A legacy is what you leave in people, and both are happening at the exact same time. One is impacting the present, while the other is impacting the future. **One generation's legacy becomes another generation's inheritance.**

Inheritance of Grace

Psalms 103: 1-5 reveals a truth that should fill all believer's hearts with joy. It says, "Praise the LORD, my soul; all my inmost being, praise his holy name. Praise the LORD, my soul, and forget not all his benefits—who forgives all your sins and heals all your diseases, who redeems your life from the pit and crowns you with love and compassion, who satisfies your desires with good things so that your youth is renewed like the eagle's.

Get excited, sons and daughters of God. You have inherited benefits. Then, it goes on to list just a few of those benefits.

He says we have forgiveness of sins, healing from diseases, the redemption of life from the pit; we are crowned with love and compassion, we will be satisfied with good things, and finally, God desires to renew our youth. These are just a few of the benefits that we have inherited as sons and daughters of the King.

Ultimately, we have inherited grace. Why grace? because without it, nothing else matters. Without grace, we would receive what we deserved, which is God's wrath. God's grace allows us to receive what we do not deserve.

Psalms 103:10-12 He does not treat us as our sins deserve or repay us according to our iniquities. For as high as the heavens are above the earth, so great is his love for those who fear him; as far as the east is from the west, so far has he removed our transgressions from us.

This passage of scripture paints pictures of landscapes that are far beyond our imagination. I believe that these pictures are painted for a reason. This type of inherited grace is hard to understand. As high as the heavens are above the earth. Our minds can only imagine what that looks like. It is beyond our comprehension. Not only does God challenge the height of our knowledge or imagination but then He challenges the width of our knowledge and imagination. The writer of Psalms 103 says regarding grace that God has given grace as far as the East is from the West. When you look at a globe there is what we call the North Pole and the South Pole. They are points in which we can begin and end. Here's a powerful thought: if God would have extended grace from north to south, it would stop. There would be a point at which grace would begin and end. In other words, at some point, we could, and we certainly would, do so much wrong that eventually, we would make our way from the North Pole of God's grace to the South Pole of God's grace. We would run out of grace.

So why did God say as far as the East is from the West? While there is a start and an end from north to south, according to scientists, this is not the case if you are going from east to west. Scientists say if you were to go from east to west, you would never find an end. You would walk in an endless circle. Psalms 103 tells us that God's love and grace are endless. **Endless grace is our inheritance.** Does this mean that we can sin freely? No! By no means am I saying this. In our pursuit to be like Christ, we will often discover that we are human and that we are in need of forgiveness and grace. In those moments, we can count on our inheritance of grace. If we are quick to repent, there will be grace that removes our sin as far from the East as is from the West. Grace is our inheritance. Do we deserve it? No! But, nonetheless, it is what our father left in the Will and Trust to us.

This is the yin and the yang of the Christian walk. We have an inheritance because of grace, and grace is our inheritance. One blessing brings with it the other. **Inheritance and grace walk hand and hand. They are married to each other.** Which is why God says that he is married to the backslider in Jeremiah 3:14-15 "Return, O backsliding children," says the Lord, "For I am married to you. I will take you, one from a city and two from a family, and I will bring you to Zion. And I will give you shepherds according to My heart, who will feed you with knowledge and understanding.

Forgiveness

The saying "to err is human, to forgive is divine" has been in use since it was coined by Alexander Pope in the early 18th century. **Unforgiveness is withholding grace. It is refusing to give the Godly inheritance that rightfully belongs to another human.** If mankind's inheritance is grace, and we have grace because of our inheritance, then who am I to steal someone's inheritance? This brings new meaning to the thought that the thief comes to steal, kill, and destroy, found in John 10:10. Satan comes to steal our inheritance of forgiveness and grace. When we decide not to forgive and steal someone else's inheritance, then we foolishly place ourselves as the head of the Will & Trust. We are not the head of the Will & Trust; we are simply inheritors. Who am I to withhold what I, too, have had to inherit, which is grace and forgiveness? Let's remember that we did not create this wealth or this kingdom; we have simply inherited it.

Joshua 24:13 states, "I gave you a land on which you had not labored and cities that you had not built, and you dwell in them. You eat the fruit of vineyards and olive orchards that you did not plant."

God was telling the Israelites and Joshua the same thing that he wants us to remember. **You did not build the kingdom; you inherited it.**

One of the most life-changing revelations that I have had has been the idea of the relationship between the cross of Christ and the inheritance of the believer.

I am learning on each mile of my Christian journey that this Christian walk is all about a father trying to give his sons and daughters an inheritance. Some of us are unaware of this inheritance. Some of us run from our inheritance. Some of us waste and squander our inheritance, while others humbly receive, believe, and walk in our inheritance.

From Genesis to Revelation, the Bible is about grace and inheritance. I have often considered the fact that God has given us a song that even the angels cannot sing. It is a song of redemption and inherited grace. It is an amazing thought that even the angels themselves cannot fathom. For they do not know what it is to inherit grace. It is a song that they cannot sing. They can see the grace that we have inherited. They act according to the assignment that our inherited grace has issued out to them, but only we can sing a heartfelt hallelujah for what inherited grace has brought into our lives. Why? Because he who has been forgiven much loves much. **Redemption song is most passionately belted out of the mouths of mankind who needed to be redeemed.**

The Hammer & The Nails

Take a journey with me to a place called Golgotha. It is also known in Greek as the place of the skull due to its shape. We believers today call it Calvary. It is the place where Christ was crucified. There were tools and symbols used that day to kill Jesus. They are the same tools and symbols that now represent our inheritance of Grace.

Jesus was not carrying a cross. He was carrying the very instrument He would use to release our inheritance. The cross was a bridge that Jesus would use as a highway for mankind to have a relationship with the Father again. It was an instrument of torture, but it was also an instrument of restoration. It was not enough for him to be willing to lay on that cross. He would have to die on it willingly. Jesus knew that his death would release our inheritance. Ultimately, **somebody has to die for your inheritance to be released.** In our world, that may be a parent or close relative. In the spiritual world, that was Jesus. The law is the law. Somebody has to die for an inheritance to be released. So Jesus followed the law and gave his life so we, his children, could receive our inheritance.

As Jesus lay on the cross, he was thinking about us and how what He was about to leave on the earth would change the world, and his death would create a world of mini Christs. The same power that would raise him from the dead would now live in us. That power would be an inheritance passed on to us.

From the moment that the hammer made the screaming sound from striking the nail, grace started to be released. With every banging sound, inheritance was being given to God's children. Bang! Grace was being released. Bang! Peace was being released. Bang! Healing was being released. Bang! Deliverance was being released. Bang! Joy was being given to God's children. Bang! Salvation was being offered to the world. Bang! Power was being given to us. Bang! Provision was released for every need. Bang! Freedom was given to the captives. Bang! Bang! Destiny was released. Bang! Purpose and dreams were released.

The demons themselves must not have read the Will and Last Testament of our Lord and Savior. If they had understood the process of inheritance, then they would have been more careful. They were better off letting Jesus live than killing him. You see, it was his death. It was that cross, that hammer, and nails, that released our inheritance. Bang! **Jesus did not just spread his arms and die; he actually was extending his hand to give us our inheritance.** Jesus followed the law and died, then he broke the law and rose again from the grave. He wanted to show us the full power of our inheritance. Just as He rose from the grave and took the sting out of death, we too could inherit the boldness to say death, where is your sting? Death has lost its power over Jesus and those who serve Him. This is our inheritance. Bang!

The Parable of the Inherited Peace

Once upon a time, in a quiet village nestled between rolling hills and lush forests, there lived a young man named Ethan. Ethan was known for his calm demeanor and unwavering peace of mind, traits that were often the subject of admiration and curiosity among the villagers.

Ethan's father, Benjamin, had been a wise and prudent man. Throughout his life, Benjamin worked hard, not only to provide for his family but also to instill values of wisdom, integrity, and foresight in his son. When Benjamin passed away, he left Ethan a substantial inheritance. However, this inheritance was not just of material wealth; it included a wealth of wisdom and principles that Benjamin had lived by.

As Ethan grew older, he faced numerous challenges. There were times when the village faced droughts, and food was scarce. There were moments when illness spread, and fear gripped the hearts of many. Yet, through all these trials, Ethan remained unshaken.

One particularly harsh winter, the village was hit by a severe storm that destroyed many homes and left the villagers in despair. While others panicked, Ethan calmly organized shelter and food for those in need, using his inheritance to support the community. He shared his resources generously, ensuring that no one went hungry or cold.

The villagers were curious about Ethan's unwavering peace and security. One day, a group of them gathered the courage to ask him, "Ethan, how is it that you remain so calm and secure, even in the face of such adversity?"

Ethan smiled and invited them to sit with him. "My dear friends," he began, "the peace and security you see in me are gifts from my father. He left me an inheritance, but it is not just the wealth that keeps me secure. My father taught me that true wealth lies in wisdom, compassion, and faith."

He continued, "My father always said that challenges are a part of life, but it is how we respond to them that defines our character. He taught me to save and prepare for tough times, to help others in need, and to trust that we can overcome any obstacle with the right mindset and actions. This is the inheritance that gives me peace of mind."

Ethan's words resonated deeply with the villagers. They realized that while material wealth can provide comfort, it is the wealth of wisdom and values that truly sustains and guides one through life's storms.

Inspired by Ethan, the villagers began to adopt the principles he shared. They worked together, helping each other, and building a community founded on mutual support, wisdom, and foresight. Over time, the village flourished, not just because of the material wealth that Ethan had shared, but because of the invaluable inheritance of wisdom and peace of mind that he had imparted.

And so, the village prospered, and Ethan's father's legacy lived on, proving that true security and peace of mind come from a heart and mind grounded in wisdom, compassion, and faith.

Living With an Inheritance Mindset

An inheritance allows you to live with peace and a sense of security that others do not have. You know there is nothing to be concerned about because your father has provided for your future. You know that your future is safe, so you live with unshakable courage in your present. Let me ask you, what would you be courageous enough to do if you knew that your future was safe? What risk would you take? What dreams would you pursue? What freedom would you walk in? Would you smile in the midst of life's storms? Would you be a pillar of peace in a world that is full of anxiety? Would you be full of faith while living on a planet that is drowning in doubt?

You need to know that the scenario that has been painted above is true of you and me. We have a Father in Heaven who has secured our future so we can live radically in the present. The word of God tells us:

Matthew 6:25-30

"Therefore I tell you, do not worry about your life, what you will eat or drink; or about your body, what you will wear. Is not life more than food, and the body more than clothes? Look at the birds of the air; they do not sow or reap or store away in barns, and yet your heavenly Father feeds them. Are you not much more valuable than they? Can any one of you by worrying add a single hour to your life? "And why do you worry about clothes? See how the flowers of the field grow. They do not labor or spin. Yet I tell you that not even Solomon in all his splendor was dressed like one of these. If that is how God clothes the grass of the field, which is here today and tomorrow is thrown into the fire, will he not much more clothe you—you of little faith?

God was challenging us to live with an inheritance mindset. There is provision today. There is provision for tomorrow. There is provision for the future. Now, we can live in radical, perfect peace in the present.

This is what God describes in Isaiah 26:3, which says: "You will keep in perfect peace those whose minds are steadfast because they trust in you."

An inheritance is what you leave with people. A legacy is what you leave in people.

CHAPTER 5

TRUST-FUND BABIES

TRUST FUND BABIES

You may not like the term, but you and I are trust fund babies. Let's look at the definition. A trust fund baby is someone whose parents have set up a trust fund (Inheritance) for them. The term is a popular cultural reference that's often used negatively. There is an idea that trust fund babies are born with silver spoons in their mouths. The term is often used negatively, implying they have an advantage and are privileged.

Both of these thoughts are true when it comes to the children of God. When we gave our lives to Christ, we were given an advantage. As Jesus was making his way to the cross, he wanted his disciples to understand the purpose of his death and resurrection. Jesus was leaving to give them an advantage. He told his disciples in John 16:7

"But I tell you the truth, **it is to your advantage** that I go away; for if I do not go away, the Helper will not come to you; but if I go, I will send Him to you."

The Helper is the Holy Spirit, the Spirit of truth, as He is referred to later in verse 13. You can call him the Helper, the Holy Spirit, or the Spirit of God. I call Him The Advantage.

We are trust fund babies because we have been given an advantage. His name is Holy Spirit. Let me ask you a question. Have you tapped into your advantage? Have you been living life without using your advantage?

You can be sure that when Satan sees us, he sees a bunch of trust fund babies. Kids with an advantage. As stated in Job 1:7-11 The LORD said to Satan, "Where have you come from?" Satan answered the LORD, "From roaming throughout the earth, going back and forth on it." Then the LORD said to Satan, "Have you considered my servant Job? There is no one on earth like him; he is blameless and upright, a man who fears God and shuns evil. Does Job fear God for nothing?" Satan replied. Have you not put a hedge around him and his household and everything he has? You have blessed the work of his hands, so that his flocks and herds are spread throughout the land.

In other words, Satan was accusing God of having a trust fund baby. He was accusing God of giving Job an advantage. What Satan was well aware of was that Job's advantage was based on how much God loved Job. What he did not count on, was how much Job loved God.

We should be humble and thankful and yet we are privileged. We have been given the privilege of entering into His presence. The honor of being able to come into the Holy of Holies. The humble thought that we can approach the throne of grace with confidence.

Hebrews 4:15-16

For we do not have a high priest who is unable to empathize with our weaknesses, but we have one who has been tempted in every way, just as we are—yet he did not sin. Let us then approach God's throne of grace with confidence so that we may receive mercy and find grace to help us in our time of need.

Does this mean that we become lazy in our walk with Christ? No! It means that we work out our salvation with fear and trembling. The Apostle Paul challenged the church of

Philippians to do this. He said Jesus had already played and won the game of life, and the victory that Jesus won made you winners. "You are winners; now win."

Philippians 2:12-13
Therefore, my dear friends, as you have always obeyed—not only in my presence but now much more in my absence—continue to work out your salvation with fear and trembling, for it is God who works in you to will and to act in order to fulfill his good purpose.

It would not make sense to start the game with a one-hundred-point lead and lose the game. Or to start the race with a one-hundred-mile lead and lose the race because we were too lazy to run. You are winners; now win!

When We Worship

When we worship, something happens. Satan hears our worship and says, "NO! Here come those trust fund babies, singing that trust fund music." Songs about God's faithfulness, power, love, mercy, and grace—trust fund baby music. When we worship, things begin to move and shake. Chains begin to break. When we worship, we remind the devil of what he used to be and had before his fall.

You know the songs, like His Eye is on the Sparrow, Amazing Grace. They are all the songs of God's trust fund babies.

True revelation should bring about a release. As I become aware of my inheritance, a new found freedom should be released in your life. The list that you are about to read is what I call the Inherited One Hundred. I pray that as you read it, it would start a Jailbreak in your life. I pray that it would cause you to break forth in worship to our God.

<u>The Inherited One Hundred</u>

1. **Eternal Life:** Through faith in Jesus Christ. (John 3:16).

2. **Salvation:** By grace through faith (Ephesians 2:8-9)

3. **Forgiveness of Sins:** Through the sacrifice of Jesus (1 John 1:9).

4. **Righteousness:** Declared righteous through faith in Jesus (Romans 3:22).

5. **Adoption into God's Family:** Adopted as children of God (Romans 8:15).

6. **Holy Spirit:** Received as a guide and comforter (John 14:26).

7. **Peace:** With God through our Lord Jesus Christ (Romans 5:1).

8. **Joy:** In the Lord (Philippians 4:4).

9. **Love:** Experiencing the unconditional love of God (Romans 5:5).

10. **Grace:** In abundance (2 Corinthians 12:9).

11. **Mercy:** New every morning (Lamentations 3:22-23).

12. **Strength:** Can do all things through Christ (Philippians 4:13).

13. **Hope:** In the promises of God (Romans 15:13).

14. **Wisdom:** Given generously by God (James 1:5).

15. **Protection:** God is our protector and shield
(Psalm 18:2).

16. **Provision:** For all our needs (Philippians 4:19).

17. **Healing:** By His stripes, we are healed
(Isaiah 53:5).

18. **Sanctification:** Through the truth of God's
word (John 17:17).

19. **Redemption:** By the blood of Christ
(Ephesians 1:7).

20. **New Creation:** Made new in Christ
(2 Corinthians 5:17).

21. **Spiritual Gifts:** For the edification of the church
(1 Corinthians 12:4-11).

22. **Fellowship:** With God and other believers
(1 John 1:3).

23. **Inheritance in Heaven:** Reserved in heaven
(1 Peter 1:4).

24. **Victory:** Over sin and death through Jesus
(1 Corinthians 15:57).

25. **Holiness:** Called to live holy lives (1 Peter 1:15-16).

26. **Purity:** Through faith in Christ (1 John 3:3).

27. **Imputed Glory:** Sharing in God's glory
(Romans 8:17).

28. **Purpose:** In Christ (Ephesians 2:10).

29. **Spiritual Armor:** Equipped with the armor of God (Ephesians 6:10-18).

30. **Freedom:** From the bondage of sin (Romans 6:18).

31. **Access to God:** Direct access through prayer (Hebrews 4:16).

32. **Citizenship in Heaven:** Our citizenship is in heaven (Philippians 3:20).

33. **Transformation:** By the renewing of our minds (Romans 12:2).

34. **Unity with Christ:** In His death and resurrection (Romans 6:5).

35. **Fruit of the Spirit:** Bearing the fruit of the Spirit (Galatians 5:22-23).

36. **Resurrection:** To eternal life (1 Corinthians 15:52).

37. **Comfort:** In times of trouble (2 Corinthians 1:3-4).

38. **Discipline:** For our good (Hebrews 12:6).

39. **Peace of God:** Guards our hearts and minds (Philippians 4:7).

40. **Inheritance of the Kingdom:** Inheriting the kingdom of God (Matthew 25:34).

41. **Guidance:** In our decisions (Proverbs 3:5-6).

42. **Spiritual Insight:** Understanding God's word (Ephesians 1:17-18).

43. **Courage:** In the face of adversity (Joshua 1:9).

44. **Justice:** God's justice and righteousness (Psalm 89:14).

45. **Contentment:** In all circumstances (Philippians 4:11-12).

46. **Security:** In God's love (Romans 8:38-39).

47. **Assurance:** Of our salvation (1 John 5:13).

48. **Spiritual Growth:** Growing in faith and knowledge of God (2 Peter 3:18).

49. **Servanthood:** Called to serve others in love (Galatians 5:13).

50. **Eternal Reward:** For our faithfulness (Revelation 22:12).

51. **Comfort in Trials:** So we can comfort others (2 Corinthians 1:4).

52. **Peace with Others:** Called to live in peace with everyone (Romans 12:18).

53. **Maturity:** Growing into maturity in Christ (Ephesians 4:13).

54. **Fruitfulness:** Bearing much fruit (John 15:5).

55. **Discernment:** Ability to discern truth from error (Hebrews 5:14).

56. **God's Presence:** Always with us (Matthew 28:20).

57. **New Heart:** Given a new heart and spirit (Ezekiel 36:26).

58. **God's Covenant:** Part of God's eternal covenant (Hebrews 13:20-21).

59. **Unfailing Love:** God's love never fails (Psalm 136).

60. **Light:** Called to be the light of the world (Matthew 5:14).

61. **Salt:** We are the salt of the earth (Matthew 5:13).

62. **Boldness:** Approaching God's throne with boldness (Hebrews 4:16).

63. **Perseverance:** Ability to persevere (James 1:12).

64. **Overcoming:** Overcomers through Christ (1 John 5:4).

65. **Christ's Intercession:** Jesus intercedes for us (Romans 8:34).

66. **New Identity:** A new identity in Christ (2 Corinthians 5:17).

67. **Sanctified Mind:** We have the mind of Christ (1 Corinthians 2:16).

68. **God's Promises:** All God's promises are "Yes" in Christ (2 Corinthians 1:20).

69. **Gift of Faith:** Received as a gift (Ephesians 2:8).

70. **Reconciliation:** Reconciled to God (2 Corinthians 5:18-19).

71. **Christ's Righteousness:** Clothed in Christ's righteousness (Philippians 3:9).

72. **Strength in Weakness:** God's power made perfect in our weakness (2 Corinthians 12:9).

73. **Interdependence:** Members of one body in Christ (Romans 12:5).

74. **Friendship with God:** Called friends of God (John 15:15).

75. **Living Hope:** Through the resurrection of Jesus (1 Peter 1:3).

76. **Joy in Trials:** Joy even in trials (James 1:2-3).

77. **Blessings:** Blessed with every spiritual blessing (Ephesians 1:3).

78. **Eternal Perspective:** Set our minds on things above (Colossians 3:2).

79. **Living Sacrifice:** Called to offer our bodies as living sacrifices (Romans 12:1).

80. **Renewed Mind:** Minds renewed through God's word (Romans 12:2).

81. **Christ's Love:** Nothing can separate us from Christ's love (Romans 8:38-39).

82. **Truth:** Sanctified by God's truth (John 17:17).

83. **God's Workmanship:** Created in Christ (Ephesians 2:10).

84. **Self-Control:** Given a spirit of self-control (2 Timothy 1:7).

85. **Generosity:** Called to be generous (2 Corinthians 9:6-7).

86. **Humility:** Called to be humble (Philippians 2:3-4).

87. **Gentleness:** Called to be gentle (Galatians 5:23).

88. **Faithfulness:** Called to be faithful (1 Corinthians 4:2).

89. **Kindness:** Called to be kind (Ephesians 4:32).

90. **Patience:** Called to be patient (Colossians 3:12).

91. **Forgiveness:** Called to forgive others (Matthew 6:14-15).

92. **Unity:** Called to unity in the body of Christ (Ephesians 4:3).

93. **Restoration:** Restored to God (Psalm 23:3).

94. **Peaceful Living:** Called to live peacefully
(Romans 12:18).

95. **Obedience:** Called to obey God's commandments
(John 14:15).

96. **Evangelism:** Called to share the gospel
(Matthew 28:19-20).

97. **Prayer:** Privilege of communicating with God
(Philippians 4:6).

98. **Worship:** Called to worship God in spirit and truth
(John 4:24).

99. **Direction:** God's word is a light to our feet
(Psalm 119:105).

100. **Weapon:** God's word is the sword of the Spirit
(Hebrews 4:12).

Your inheritance in Christ is not imaginary; it's the real thing, and it's to be lived out.

CHAPTER 6

UNCLAIMED INHERITANCE

Monuments

We all want to be remembered. We all want to leave something for the next generation, whether that be finances, faith, or core values. However, there are situations that leave some of us with a lifetime of knowledge, wealth, and faith but no one to leave it with when we are gone. You may have never met the right person in life and never married. Maybe you married but were unable to have children. Maybe just the dynamics and setup of your family have left you on your deathbed with no one to leave what you have built over your lifetime. You have gathered, but there is no one to hand the basket to. The estate company pulls into a home full of treasures and places a price tag on the most valuable things that you have accumulated over your life, only to sell them for less than half the price to a stranger. A stranger who does not know that the blanket that they just bought at your estate sale was hand-knitted by your great-grandmother. Or that the two dollars that they just spent to buy that fishing pole actually was the fishing pole that your gandfather used to show you how to fish. They don't know that the beautiful ring they got for a mere twenty dollars was once wrapped around the finger of your mother and was a symbol of love during her fifty-year marriage to your father. Or the blue kiddy pool they are stuffing in the back of their minivan is the same pool your children made memories with in the backyard on hot sunny days. The kids played while you sat in the lawn chair and sipped lemonade.

 I would dare to say that very few people, if any at all, actually desire to live a life where they gave nothing or had nothing to offer after a life well lived. Yet this was the case for a young man by the name of Absalom, the son of King David. We find his last Will and Testament in 2 Samuel 18:18. During his lifetime, Absalom had taken a pillar and erected it in the King's Valley as a monument to himself, for he thought, "I have no son to carry on the memory of my name." He named the pillar after himself, and it is called Absalom's Monument to this day.

This is the process of mankind to this day. When we have no one to inherit what we have built, we build monuments to ourselves.

Unused & Untapped

If you die without any relatives to inherit your money, the state will typically receive your assets, a process called "escheat" pronounced (s-cheat). This is where the government takes ownership of your property because no identifiable heirs can be found; this happens when you die without a Will or if you have no surviving family members. It all goes to the government. Sitting in some storage room unused. Raffled off for pennies. It was handled with a lack of honor by its new owners, who have no idea of the price that was paid or the history behind each item.

Imagine with me, if you would, living a life where you never walk in all God has left for you. Imagine the ultimate price of God's son being crucified on a cross and giving gifts unto men only to have mankind ignore what has been given. The gifts were given but left unused, dishonored, and devalued. Gifts left to return to the heavens.

Famous Motivational Speaker Les Brown changed my life many years ago when I heard him give a speech where he painted the following picture.

"Imagine you're on your deathbed—and standing around your bed are the ghosts representing your unfilled potential. The ghosts of the ideas you never acted on. The ghosts of the talents you didn't use. And they're standing around your bed. Angry. Disappointed. Upset. 'We came to you because you could have brought us to life,' they say. 'And now we go to the grave together.'"

 So I ask you today: How many ghosts are going to be around your bed when your time comes? How much of your inheritance will you leave on the table of the earth? My mother used to tell us that we could not leave the dinner table until our plates were empty. As an adult, this is my model. I refuse to leave the table of this earth until my plate is empty. Until I tap into and use all of my inheritance. Until I become all that God has called me to be. I press toward the high call of Christ. I press toward the high call of my inheritance.

God has always desired to have a family. According to scripture, he made that family in His image. He went as far as to claim the Israelites as his own people. They were his sons and daughters. He has always longed to leave an inheritance.

It is the very reason in the Old Testament that his spirit came upon people. In the New Testament, his spirit dwelt within people. The Holy Spirit came upon and dwelt in sons and daughters. With every miracle and prophetic word, they were walking in their inheritance. It was the reason that Jesus died so that His sons and daughters could inherit the kingdom.

In the physical, I will not leave any of my inheritance for the government to gather. In the spirit, I will not leave a room full of inherited gifts, talents, abilities, anointing, unused and untapped. As the old gospel spiritual song said, "God is trying to tell you something." I would add God is not only trying to tell you something, but He is trying to give you something. God is trying to give you your inheritance.

Fight For It

They were known as The Daughters of Zelophehad. Their names were Mahlah, Noah, Hoglah, Milkah and Tirzah. They were five young women who fought for their inheritance. The book of Numbers 27:1-11 tells their courageous story.

Numbers 27:1-11

The daughters of Zelophehad son of Hepher, the son of
Gilead, the son of Makir, the son of Manasseh, belonged to
the clans of Manasseh son of Joseph. The names of the
daughters were Mahlah, Noah, Hoglah, Milkah and Tirzah.
They came forward and stood before Moses, Eleazar the
priest, the leaders and the whole assembly at the entrance to
the tent of meeting and said, "Our father died in the
wilderness. He was not among Korah's followers, who
banded together against the LORD, but he died for his own
sin and left no sons. Why should our father's name disappear
from his clan because he had no son? Give us property among
our father's relatives." So Moses brought their case before the
LORD, and the LORD said to him, "What Zelophehad's
daughters are saying is right. You must certainly give them
property as an inheritance among their father's relatives and
give their father's inheritance to them. "Say to the Israelites,
'If a man dies and leaves no son, give his inheritance to his
daughter. If he has no daughter, give his inheritance to his
brothers. If he has no brothers, give his inheritance to his
father's brothers. If his father had no brothers, give his
inheritance to the nearest relative in his clan, that he may

possess it. This is to have the force of law for the Israelites, as the LORD commanded Moses.' "

The five daughters of Zelophehad fought for their inheritance. The question is, will you fight for yours? They had no legal right to inheritance. They were disqualified for several reasons, one of them being their gender. What would give them the courage to fight for the inheritance of their father? I personally believe that it was their mindset, honor, and future vision. Let's talk about this for a minute.

Mindset: This portion of scripture starts out by telling us that while these young women were certainly a part of the Israelite people, they were also a part of another people group who thought differently. A people who had a different mindset. A culture where women were not looked down upon but honored as equals. It says they were of the tribe of Manasseh, which belonged to the clans of Manasseh, the son of Joseph. According to scripture, their mother, Asenath (Genesis 41:50-52) was married to Joseph. She was Egyptian. According to history, Egyptian women were treated with a level of dignity, respect, and equality unseen in many cultures. In other words, they were raised with the core values that they were not less. They were just as valuable as any male counterpart. They had a mindset to fight for what their father had left them.

What can we learn from these five courageous women? That we are not less. That the enemy will have every reason as to why we are not worthy of the inheritance that our Father God has left for us. Our sins. Our shortcomings. Yet, God says to stand and ask for your inheritance anyway. You have not, because you ask not James 4:2-3

Honor: One of the Ten Commandments is to honor your father and your mother so that your life (Inheritance) might be a long life (Exodus 20:12). The five daughters of Zelophehad honored their father. They would not let him be forgotten, even with his flaws. They would not allow what he had built in his lifetime to be lost, even in his shortcomings. Not only Moses and Eleazar, the priest, were moved by these five women, but apparently God was as well.

Future vision: They fought for their inheritance by thinking about the future generations to come. The inherited future of their family was about to be lost. Out of all the tribes and clans, their children, grandchildren, and great-grandchildren would have lived a much different life had their mothers not had a vision for their family. They thought beyond themselves and fought for something bigger; they fought for the future. We find out later in Scripture that these ladies not only spoke up, but then they executed a plan of marriage that would make sure that their inheritance would not be lost for them or their future generations. They had short-term goals and long-term plans.

Are you thinking about the future generations of your family's spiritual inheritance and the long-term impact that you can have?

The Impact: Moses brought their case before the LORD, and the LORD said to him, **"What Zelophehad's daughters are saying is right. You must certainly give them property as an inheritance among their father's relatives and give their father's inheritance to them.** "Say to the Israelites, 'If a man dies and leaves no son, give his inheritance to his daughter. If he has no daughter, give his inheritance to his brothers. If he has no brothers, give his inheritance to his father's brothers. If his father had no brothers, give his inheritance to the nearest relative in his clan, that he may possess it.

God himself said what every woman likes to hear. God said, "What Zelophehad's daughters are saying is right." Their right to the inheritance was confirmed by divine direction.

There was not only a change in the law for the five daughters of Zelophehad but it changed for everyone. God moved from declaring that they would receive an inheritance to how other generations after them would receive an inheritance. You no longer had to be a son to get it. You simply had to be next of kin. And it did not matter how far down next of kin you were as long as you were next of kin. The goal was to make sure that you got your inheritance. God said if a man dies and he has no son, give it to his brave daughters. If he has no daughters, give it to his brothers or sisters. If he has no brothers or sisters, give it to his uncle or aunts. If he has no uncle or aunts, give it to his nearest relatives of any gender. If he or she is related, pass the inheritance along.

In other words, women, men, young boys, and girls, not just in the tribe of Manasseh, but all the tribes would now be impacted. These five women made life better for everyone. Their bold stance in fighting for their inheritance became a blessing for generations to come.

In the same manner that the five daughters of Zelophehad's inheritance blessed others, we too can be a blessing to others. When other people see you walking in your inheritance, it will cause them to hunger for their inheritance as well. When people see you walking in peace, joy, freedom, and hope, they will be inspired to fight for their peace, joy, freedom, and hope as well.

The Poet Marianne Williamson says it best in this excerpt of her well-known poem (Our Deepest Fear). "We are all meant to shine, as children do. We were born to make manifest the glory of God that is within us. It's not just in some of us; it's in everyone. And as we let our own light shine, we unconsciously give other people permission to do the same. As we are liberated from our own fear, our presence automatically liberates others."

Fight for your inheritance. Walk in your inheritance and watch it liberate others to step into their inheritance.

CHAPTER 7

IT's NEVER TOO LATE

Give Me This Mountain

If you're reading this book and thinking about all the things that you have missed and the inheritance that you have not tapped into. I did not write this book to condemn believers; I wrote this book to encourage my brothers and sisters. What I want you to know is that it's never too late to claim what is yours in Christ Jesus. Go to the lost and found and claim that which is yours.

The well-known man of God, Caleb, reminds us of this timeless truth in the book of Joshua as the Israelites are heading into the Promised Land.

Joshua 14:7-14

I (Caleb) was forty years old when Moses the servant of the LORD sent me from Kadesh Barnea to explore the land. And I brought him back a report according to my convictions, but my fellow Israelites who went up with me made the hearts of the people melt in fear. I, however, followed the LORD my God wholeheartedly. So on that day, Moses swore to me, 'The land on which your feet have walked will be **your inheritance and that of your children forever** because you have followed the LORD my God wholeheartedly.' "Now then, just as the LORD promised, he has kept me alive for forty-five years since the time he said this to Moses while Israel moved about in the wilderness. **So here I am today, eighty-five years old! I am still as strong today as the day Moses sent me out**; I'm just as vigorous to go out to battle now as I was then. **Now give me this mountain that the LORD promised me that day**. You yourself heard then that the Anakites were there and their cities were large and fortified, but, the LORD helping me, I will drive them out just as he said." **Then Joshua blessed Caleb son of Jephunneh and gave him Hebron as his inheritance**. So Hebron has belonged to Caleb son of Jephunneh the Kenizzite ever since, because he followed the LORD, the God of Israel, wholeheartedly.

Caleb admitted that he was eighty-five years old. He had spent forty-five years without the inheritance, only a promise of what would be given. Maybe you are reading this book, and you can see yourself in Caleb's shoes. You know what God spoke, but you have gone so long without the manifestation that, unlike Caleb, it has left you doubting.

Caleb acknowledged his disability, which was his age. Then Caleb confessed God's ability by professing that God would keep his word and that he was able to take the mountain of his inheritance. Let me encourage you; you, too, are well able to take the mountain of your inheritance as well. It's not too late. Bow your head in prayer and declare what type of life you will live from this point forward. A life where you walk in the inherited power, grace, and love of God. A life where you will no longer allow Satan to blind you to the truths of who God says that you are as a child of God.

How To Walk In Your Inheritance

I have made it very clear that God has left us an inheritance and desires that we walk in it. I hope you have become hungry for what the Father has left for you. I also hope that you have become angry as to what the enemy has tried to steal from you. Just as Christ said, The enemy only comes to steal, kill, and destroy (John 10:10). Steal what? Your inheritance. So the question is, how do I take my mountain? How do I walk in my inheritance? Yup, this is the tipping point. This is the part where I talk about the everyday Christian life. **Victory for the believer is found in the everyday things.**

Prayer

The secret weapon of heaven is prayer. The longer I walk with Christ, the more I realize that prayer is a habit that most of us struggle with. We know to pray, and we have been told to have a prayer life, but few of us make it a habit.

We live in a world that moves at the speed of light, and so we live at the speed of light. Yet, prayer is the only thing that can actually supernaturally control that light. Prayer requires that we slow down to meet with the God of the universe. The same God who created the sun, moon, and the stars themselves. In Joshua 10, God literally made the sun stand still. He controlled the light and the speed of the light.

Joshua10:12-14 On the day the Lord gave the Amorites over
to Israel, Joshua said to the Lord in the presence of Israel:
"Sun, stand still over Gibeon, and you, moon, over the Valley
of Aijalon." So the sun stood still, and the moon stopped, till
the nation avenged itself on its enemies, as it is written in the
Book of Jashar. The sun stopped in the middle of the sky and
delayed going down about a full day. There has never been a
day like it before or since, a day when the Lord listened to a
human being. Surely, the Lord was fighting for Israel!

The inherited power of prayer. Many times, the Bible
mentions that Christ slipped away to pray. He often chose the
solitude of prayer over people. The Bible records Jesus
praying and withdrawing to pray in many places, such as:

The Mountain: Jesus prayed on the mountainside before the
sermon on the mount after multiplying loaves of bread and
fish (Luke 9:10-17).

The Wilderness: Jesus withdrew to the wilderness to pray
(Luke 5:16)

The Garden: Jesus prayed in the garden of Gethsemane before his death (Mathew 26:36-56).

The Sea: Jesus prayed by the sea (Matthew 14:22-33).

The Cross: Yes, Christ prayed on the cross (Luke 22:34).

He was showing the disciples that their inheritance must be pursued in prayer. Likewise, our inheritance must be pursued in prayer.

God's Word

God's word is his living Will and Testament. It tells us what He did and what He left us. **If you don't know the word of God, then you don't have a clue as to what your inheritance is.** You have read the Inherited One hundred in this book. They are all from God's word. This is just one hundred things, but there are many other things that you have inherited from God. It is up to us to study the bible like we are on a treasure hunt to discover who we are and who God is. The Bible is not just the word of God. It is the promises of God. You need to know that **God's promises are God's guarantees.**

In Matthew 4:1-11 as Christ was being tempted in the wilderness, with every temptation that the devil brought, Christ consistently said, "It is written." What was Jesus doing in that moment? He was saying to the devil, I know the word of God. I know that what you're trying to offer me is something that is already part of my inheritance. You cannot give me what I already own. It is written! It is my inheritance.

Fasting

In Matthew 6:17-18 Jesus said, "**When you fast**, put oil on your head and wash your face, so that it will not be obvious to others that you are fasting, but only to your Father, who is unseen; and **your Father, who sees what is done in secret, will reward you.**

Notice Jesus said WHEN you fast, not IF you fast. Let me remind you that Christ was also fasting in the wilderness (Matthew 4:1-11). Once, when Jesus' disciples were trying to cast out a demon, they were unsuccessful, and they asked Christ why they couldn't cast the demon out (Mark 9:14–29). Jesus replied, "Some only come out through fasting and prayer." In other words, **some of our inheritance must be tapped into through FASTING and prayer.**

Forgiveness

Unforgiveness stops the flow of our inheritance. God wants us to understand that a part of our inheritance is forgiveness received and given. Matthew 6:14-15 states, "If you do not forgive others their sins, your Father in heaven will not forgive your sins." Freely you have received, freely you must give.

It is a prideful thing for mankind to walk in unforgiveness when it has been forgiven so much. It tells God that we have forgotten where he found us. He found us in the dark and brought us to the light. Yet, we live as if the opposite is true. We don't have forgiveness because we deserve it. We have forgiveness because it was given to us on the cross of Christ as an inheritance to the sons and daughters of God.

Courage

God repeatedly told Joshua to be courageous. Joshua 1:9 Have I not commanded you? Be strong and courageous. Do not be afraid; do not be discouraged, for the LORD your God will be with you wherever you go."

Why would it take courage to walk in your inheritance? Because you may face some enemies along the way? Yes. But also because you will need to be careful not to fear people along the way. Not just your enemies but your frenemies. What are frenemies? People who don't want the best for you. People who are not hungry to walk in their inheritance and try to hold you back from yours. They are just as dangerous as your enemies, and maybe more. Why? Your enemies have made themselves very clear and visible. You know who they are and what they have come to do; you are careful not to allow that to happen. Your frenemies have gone to spy out the Promised Land with you but have come back with an absolutely different opinion than you. They are sure you can't take the land, but you think you can. They are sure you will lose, but you are sure that with God's help, you will win. The moment you decide to move out and experience your inheritance like Job's friends, they will begin to speak against you. Typically, this leaves you somewhat confused because you were sure these were friends. This is when you will need to be just as courageous as you were against your enemies and run toward your inheritance anyway. It takes courage to move enemies out of your way, and it takes courage to leave your frenemies behind. Your inheritance is worth it.

Humility

A child with an inheritance who has a heart full of pride is a danger to the world. They are selfish, entitled, and, if I could say it, useless hoarders. God says in Micah 6:8 He has shown you, O man, what is good; And what does the LORD require of you But to do justly, To love mercy, And to walk humbly with your God?

A child with an inheritance who has a heart full of humility is a blessing to the world. This is the child that the three wise men found in the manger as they followed the north star. A humble child with an inheritance who was born to be a blessing to the world. This is our model of humility. It is a humble heart that allows our inheritance to flow like a river. This is what Christ was referring to when he said, "Give, and it will be given to you. A good measure, pressed down, shaken together, and running over, will be poured into your lap. For with the measure you use, it will be measured to you." Luke 6:38. **Humility allows your inheritance to be a blessing to you as well as others.**

If you have not noticed, these are not profound truths; they're just truths we have struggled to live. The gospel was never meant to be complicated. It was a hard sacrifice with a simple truth. For God so loved the world that he gave his sons and daughters an inheritance. Even the act of receiving Christ as your Lord and Savior is elementary and yet the most important decision you will ever make in your life. We know the process: Ask, Believe, Confess, and Receive. Ask Christ into your Heart. Believe that Jesus died on the cross for your sins and rose again on the third day. Confess that you are a sinner who needs a savior and receive Christ as your king! For most of us, this was a hard decision but a simple process.

Could it be that God never wanted us to fail at becoming or having all that he wanted for us? Could it be that God longs for us actually to walk in our inheritance? I think so. God desires for us to spend eternity in heaven. The father longs to give us the keys to the kingdom. The keys are part of our inheritance. They unlock rooms of revelation, rooms of gifts, talents, and abilities that God has set aside for us as his children. Grab your keys, and let's go. Let's find out what this chain full of keys actually unlocks. Remember, he said keys (Plural), not key (Singular). Spend your life enjoying the many rooms that can be unlocked with your inherited kingdom keys. Remember, it's never too late!

CHAPTER 8

HOW TO LOSE
YOUR INHERITANCE

Ineligible For Inheritance

What would make one ineligible for their inheritance? According to the law: If someone is involved in your death, such as by committing murder or manslaughter, they would generally be ineligible to inherit any part of your estate due to the legal principle that "no one should profit from their crime.". This means that even if you named them as a beneficiary in your Will, the court would likely deem them ineligible to receive any part of their inheritance. In layman's terms, if you are involved in my death intentionally or unintentionally, you are legally out of the Will.

Becoming aware of this law has opened my eyes to the scriptures in a new way. It has made me more thankful and filled my heart with gratitude for what Christ did for us on the cross. It made me realize that Jesus didn't just die for us; Jesus also fought for us.

Keep Us In The Will

Some laws must be followed. You cannot take up residence on Earth without having an Earth suit known as a body. When you die, you must leave this Earth suit; therefore, you can no longer reside on planet Earth. Even Jesus had to put on an Earth suit to walk on Earth as a man. He followed the law, was born a child, and grew in favor with God and man.

Let's revisit the law and walk through the love of God. If you are responsible for someone's death intentionally or unintentionally, you can no longer remain in the will; you lose your inheritance.

It is a humbling thought to realize that when Jesus was standing before Pilate in John 10:18 and said, "No one takes my life from me, but I lay it down of my own accord. I have authority to lay it down and authority to take it up again. This command I received from my Father."

What Pilate didn't know is that Christ was following the law. Out of love for Pilate, Jesus said… No man takes my life… Pilate didn't take my life; I freely laid it down. He was saying

God keep Pilate in the Will just in case he decides to receive me and tap into his inheritance. Jesus was trying to save Pilate's life. Do you mean Jesus loved Pilate? Yes! Jesus was saying, "Keep him in the Will." Had he allowed Pilate to be responsible for his death, it would mean that Pilate was out of the Will. Remember what Jesus's mission was, it was to seek and save the lost.

When Malchus, the slave who spied on Jesus and who led the Roman soldiers to the location of Jesus, had his ear cut off by Peter. Jesus reached down and healed his ear. What was he saying? Father, don't hold him responsible for my death. Keep him in the Will. How does it feel to have the man that you betrayed turn around and heal you? How does it feel to have him fight for your eternity and inheritance while you try to terminate his existence?

When Judas betrayed Christ with a kiss, Jesus looked at him and said do what you have to do, friend, Jesus called him friend. In other words, Father, keep him in the Will. It was not God's desire for Judas to take his own life. When Peter denied Christ three times. Jesus showed up after his resurrection and had a conversation with Peter. He wanted

Peter to know this was not your fault; you're still in the Will. When the Roman soldiers beat him thirty-nine times with a whip, pulled his beard out of his face, placed a crown of thorns on his head, mocked him, and hung him to die. Jesus was hung between two thieves. One mocked him, and the other acknowledged who he was. Then, he asked Jesus to remember him. While dying on the cross, Jesus pushed pause on his mission and spoke directly to this man, saying, "Today you will be in heaven with me." In other words, you are in the Will. As Jesus in his last moments, says, "Father, forgive them, for they know not what they do (Luke 23:34). What did Jesus mean by this statement? "Father, keep them in the Will!" They don't know what they are doing. They don't know that if they are responsible for my death, they can't receive the inheritance that I came to give to them. So into your hands, I commit, or I give my spirit. I give my spirit. **They have not taken my life; I give my life.** This way, they all stay in the Will and have a chance to know me as Lord and Savior. Keep them in the Will, Father! Keep them in the Will! **Everything Jesus did was to keep us in the Will.**

How often do we, as children of God, find ourselves down and discouraged? How many times in your Christian walk have you fallen short of the glory of God only to spend hours, days, and weeks beating yourself up for your failure? Let me remind you that if Christ can forgive the people who put him on the cross, he can forgive you. If Christ can keep them in the Will, he can keep you in the Will.

He Broke The Law

Some laws are meant to be broken. Revelation 1:18 I am He that liveth, and was dead; and behold, I am alive for evermore, Amen, and have the keys of hell and of death. Yes, Jesus was an outlaw. He broke the law for me and you to make sure that we could receive our inheritance.

Death once had a sting and a victory that was final. But after Christ followed the law by dying in order to fight death, he broke the law by defeating death and rising from death.

1 Corinthians 15:55-57 O death, where is thy sting? O grave, where is thy victory? The sting of death is sin, and the

strength of sin is the law. But thanks be to God, which giveth us the victory through our Lord Jesus Christ.

According to the Bible, Jesus performed over forty miracles. According to the disciple John, there were many miracles that were not recorded.

John 21:25 states: There are also many other things that Jesus did. Were every one of them to be written, I suppose that the world itself could not contain the books that would be written.

Based on Webster's Dictionary, a miracle can be defined as an extraordinary event manifesting divine intervention in human affairs. This tells us that Jesus was constantly breaking the laws of nature so that his children could experience their inheritance.

Jesus broke the law when his mother asked him to turn water into wine. But for his mother, He defied the law and honored his mother's request. He showed us all that part of our inheritance was ask, and you shall receive, knock, and the door will be open (Matthew 7:7-8).

Jesus broke the law when he healed the man who had a withered hand on the sabbath in Matthew 12:9-13. He allowed that man to experience his inheritance on the Sabbath, and people were angry. I believe that the enemy was not just angry about the day he was healed on. I believe that the enemy was more angry about the revelation that this man received. A revelation that released a portion of his inheritance, which was healing.

Jesus broke the law for Jairus. Jesus allowed his daughter to die so he could raise her from the dead to be glorified (Mark 5). Jairus tapped into his inheritance. Jesus broke the law for Lazarus by calling his name from amongst the dead, and Lazarus came back to life.

Jesus broke the law when he got involved in an extraordinary event that manifested divine intervention in human affairs for the woman with the issue of blood.

Matthew 9:20-22 And, behold, a woman, which was diseased with an issue of blood twelve years, came behind him, and touched the hem of his garment: for she said within herself, If I may but touch his garment, I shall be whole. But Jesus turned him about, and when he saw her, he said, Daughter, be of good comfort; thy faith hath made thee whole. And the woman was made whole from that hour. Tapped into her inheritance.

As you can see, **it has never been God's desire for us to become ineligible for our inheritance.** It has always been God's heart that we remain eligible for inheritance. Now, let's go back to the cross and hear the love of God as Jesus says, "Father, forgive them, for they know not what they do." **Father, keep them in the Will. Father, keep them eligible for their inheritance.**

A Bike For a Knife

It was absolutely beautiful. It was a chrome Huffy bike. My single-parent mom worked hard and made great sacrifices to get her little boy the one thing he wanted that year: transportation. At eight years old, I had just become the coolest kid on the block. I was the cool kid with the cool bike.

As I went out to ride my bike that day, my mother commanded me not to leave my block. So, with all the excitement that an eight-year-old could muster up, I sped from one end of my inner city block to the next. The best days were when cars came by, and I could race them on my bike. Even better, because we lived across the street from the railroad tracks, they were my ultimate challenge when he trains came. The train would let off a loud horn sound, letting the residential neighborhood know that it was coming through and that we should clear the tracks. For me, that was the sound that meant the battle was on. I would beat that train from one end of my block to the other. I sat there waiting like a sped-racer, and when that 30-car train would enter my neighborhood, like the Indy Five Hundred, I competed. I went from zero to one hundred in a matter of seconds. The race was on.

With every stroke of my paddles, I built up speed and believed I could win every race. My bike was special. It made me feel like I had superpowers. I had access to things and places that I would have never had without that bike. More than that, I was confident I could win because of my bike. My huffy was my superpower.

One day, as I headed out the door to ride my bike. My mother said again, 'Stay on this block." I ran to my bike, jumped on it, and sped towards the end of my block, and just when I was about to stop and turn around like my mother had commanded, my curiosity got the best of me. It was not that my breaks didn't work anymore or that a simple turn of my handlebars would not have turned me around and kept me in the direction my mother asked me to obey. I was convinced that the grass was greener on the other side.

Instead of turning around, I rode my bike through what I thought was a barrier, but I found out it was a safety net. Like Simba in The Lion King, I headed into the Badlands. I decided to take a trip around the corner. I figured I was so fast on my bike that my mother would never know I was gone or disobeyed her command.

As I was making my way around the block, I noticed some older kids who were hanging out on a porch in front of a house. Maybe worse is that they noticed me or shall I say they noticed my bike.

Within minutes, I had made my way around the block and was sitting back in front of my house. Mission accomplished. I disobeyed my mom and saw the world on my beautiful Huffy bike.

It wasn't long before I noticed some older boys coming down the street. They just happen to be the older boys who saw me on my bike wet. I took my trip around the block. They circled around me as they approached me, singing the praises of my beautiful, cool, chrome Huffy bike. One of the boys even decided to sit on my bike. I could see the envy in his eyes. Just when. Though he was going to get up and leave, he pulled out a large pocket knife. Yes, I was scared. He flipped the blade out, showing me how shiny it was. Turned it around and showed me the broken wooden handle and made me an offer I could not refuse. He said, "I am going to take this bike, and in return, I am going to give you my knife. It's an even trade." Like a scared little boy, I took the deal—a rusted, broken-handle switchblade for a beautiful chrome Huffy bike. Translated, I am taking your bike or I am kicking your butt, you decide. I took the switchblade and watched the young man ride off into the sunset on my bike. I never saw it again. I had some explaining to do. When I entered the house, my mother asked me where my bike was, and I told her I had traded it for a rusty switchblade. Needless to say, it was not a good day. I was reminded in many ways that day of the price in sweat equity that was paid. Not to mention that I was disciplined for going where I was told not to go. My mother was upset that I disobeyed her and just as hurt that I didn't appreciate what she had given me. I guess you can say I didn't cherish what I had.

Trading For Trash

So what does this story have to do with our spiritual inheritance? Everything!

We have been given a beautiful Spiritual inheritance. Like my single-parent mom, our God has made great sacrifices to give his children the one thing that they needed, which was a savior to die of our sins. Salvation is an inheritance. Nothing on our own makes us great; it is only God and what we have inherited as children of the kingdom.

The Father has asked that we obey, trust, and love Him in return. He has asked that we cherish and do not treat lightly the spiritual inheritance that He has left for us.

Often, we listen to our flesh, leading us to stroll around the block believing that the grass is greener on the other side. **We forget that wherever there is green grass, there is also a high water bill.**

Failing to obey God and not cherishing our inheritance as believers can only lead to us trading gold for trash. If we keep playing games with God and ignoring the value of what He left us, then we too will soon watch the enemy ride off into the sunset with what was once ours. We will find ourselves standing there holding trash. My brothers and sisters, this is not an even trade. The apostle Paul speaks of our glorious inheritance in

Romans 8:18: For I consider that the sufferings of this present time are not worth comparing with the glory that is to be revealed to us.

Paul was saying, "I will not trade my inheritance for the garbage of this world."

> *We are all gifted.*
>
> *That is our inheritance.*
>
> *(Ethel Waters)*

CHAPTER 9

INHERITANCE DISPUTES

Inheritance Disputes

 Inheritance disputes between siblings and other family members can strain family relationships and set everyone on edge. We all know of a family that was strong until a loved one passed away, and the kids started to fight over the inheritance. It's enough to make anyone turn over in their grave. Thank God the grave of Christ is empty; otherwise, he just might.

I would like to say that this type of foolishness only occurs in ungodly families, but that wouldn't be true. The truth is, this foolish behavior is displayed even in the body of Christ. Jesus died, rose again, and left his children an inheritance that we spend most of our time fighting over. The enemy loves it.

We spend countless hours debating over scriptures while the world is dying and on its way to hell. But we want to be known as theologians instead of compassionate believers who win lost souls.

We spend more time and effort putting other denominations down than we do lifting Jesus up. We envy others for their gifts, talents, anointing, and abilities, and we wonder why God blessed them more than he has blessed us. Why did God seem to give them a better or bigger inheritance or spiritual gifts than the one he gave me? Why is my portion of the inheritance so small? Why do they sing better, look better, lead better, dance better, jump higher, have a bigger ministry, a better family or marriage? Why do they seem wiser or get to have the life that they have? Why is their inheritance better than mine? **We are stuck in inheritance disputes while the world is crying out for Jesus. We have ignored their cry for help while we fight over the stuff that our father left for us.**

Inheritance disputes within the body of Christ have left brothers and sisters and spiritual siblings with strained relationships. We argue over praise and worship instead of remembering that God took the right from the devil to do this according to Isaiah 14:12-14 and gave it to us as an inheritance. Yet, we would rather fight over how to do it instead of actually becoming one, lifting a beautiful sound, and doing it. We are stuck in inheritance disputes.

We argue over the Sabbath, whether we should rest on Saturday or Sunday, while mass shootings ravage our nation Monday through Friday. We fight over politics and race while the church is being labeled as self-centered, powerless, and racist.

We debate if healing is still for today until we are sick, and we want the inheritance to save our life or that of one of our loved ones. When we need it, we believe it, but when we don't, we waste our time disputing over it. Convenient Christianity is what I call this.

Mega churches look down on Micro churches, and Micro churches look down on mega-churches over inheritance. How many people attend your church? Just the names Mega and Micro make me laugh. The question isn't how large or small your church is but whether you are fulfilling your mission as a body of believers in the city you live in.

The enemy's consistent trick throughout history is to divide and conquer, and he typically does this to families when it comes to their inheritance as well. Why? Because he knows that one can chase a thousand, and two can put ten thousand to flight" (Deuteronomy 32:30). **Division is the enemy's way of making sure you don't slay or put your ten thousand to flight.**

Stop The Fighting

Like many parents, my wife and I have always challenged our children to respect and love one another. Reminding them that we, as their parents, will not always be with them. We remind them that the four of them are all they've got. They must stick together as a team. You are all you got!

When we fight each other, we all lose. Jesus made this clear in the following:

Matthew 12:26 "Every kingdom divided against itself will be ruined, and every city or household divided against itself will not stand. If Satan drives out Satan, he is divided against himself.

If we keep fighting, we will all lose. The world is watching the kingdom, and they know that race and politics can cause us to act just like them. We start fighting, and the acts of the flesh show up as stated in

Galatians 5:20-21… hatred, discord, jealousy, fits of rage, selfish ambition, dissensions, factions, and envy…

The following are real-life stories of children who fought over inheritance.

Fred Koch, co-founder of energy conglomerate Koch Industries, was worth $5.6 billion when he died. His four sons spent nearly twenty years feuding with one another over whether two brothers, Charles and David, cheated the other two, William and Frederick. After years of fighting and legal fees, they finally sold their shares in Koch Industries in 1983 for $1 billion. For many years, the billionaire brothers reportedly only communicated through lawyers, occasionally trying to humiliate and discredit one another publicly. After years of fighting and millions of dollars spent on legal fees, the brothers reconciled in 2001.

Baseball legend Ted Williams inheritance dispute is very interesting. His three children were feuding over his body. In 1996, Williams signed a will stating that he wished to be cremated and to have his ashes spread out at sea. After his death, however, the executor of his estate claimed that Williams wanted to be cryogenically frozen. Two of his children supported this action, citing a piece of paper Williams had signed in which the three all agreed to be frozen so that they would, according to an article from the AP, "be able to be together in the future, even if it is only a chance." His eldest daughter fought against the idea of Ted's body being frozen but gave up after running out of money. Ted Williams is currently frozen, with his head separated from his body. His son died of leukemia in 2004 and was also frozen.

Myra Clark Gaines' fight over an enormous inheritance is still the longest-running civil lawsuit in American history, taking over 60 years to find some kind of resolution finally. The United States Supreme Court called her case "the most remarkable in the records." From 1834 to 1891, Gaines was at the center of a legal battle to recognize her as the sole heir of her deceased father's estate and recover valuable land in New Orleans. During its 60-year history in the courtroom, the

Gaines cases appeared before the Supreme Court seventeen times and the Louisiana state and federal court at least seventy times.

Leona Helmsley, a real estate mogul in New York, was worth an estimated $4 billion when she died. She didn't like her kids or her grandkids, so she left her inheritance to her eight-year-old dog. This launched an inheritance dispute. She left no money for her grandchildren. Once the news was announced, there were so many death threats against the dog that it began requiring $100,000 worth of security each year for the protection of the dog. When the dog eventually died, the remainder of the money was given to charity.

The extreme lengths that some people go to in the heat of an inheritance dispute were demonstrated in a case involving the Wolf family. A family of two sisters and a brother who fought over an inheritance. The feud began following the death of their parents, who were valued at $3 million dollars. Fighting broke out immediately as the children sought to maximize their inheritance. The brother, in particular, seemed willing to do anything to increase his share of the family fortune.

Things got really crazy when one of the sisters was seriously injured when a box of candy that came in the mail blew up in her face as she opened it. The box was filled with pieces of pipe-glass, tacks, and other explosives. The second sister was also targeted for murder. It was only later that the brother was connected to the plot. He apparently tried to hire an ex-convict to kill his sisters to secure as much of the inheritance as possible.

Do these stories sound as crazy to you as they do to me? I think we all can agree that these are crazy stories. Yet, the same selfishness is seen in God's children around the world. We fight over inheritance, making fools of ourselves before the world. We might not fight for millions of dollars, but we will spend countless years debating the resurrection and heaven. It does not matter to me so much as to when Christ is coming back as much as it does that I am ready when he returns. This means I wake up, and I work my salvation out with fear and trembling. I do not know when I will leave the earth in the rapture or the day that I will die. What I do know is that I love God, and when he calls me home, I will be ready. We don't have time to argue about the measure of gifts, grace, and revelation that God has given to others. When we do this, it means that we are not fully focused on tapping into the full measure of gifts, grace, and revelation that God has given us. God has an inheritance for us all. Make him a proud father who has left a Will and Trust that is lived out perfectly without arguing or envy amongst his children. **Stop the fighting and start the living!**

The 12 Tribes of Israel

The 12 Tribes of Israel were the twelve sons of Jacob. Their names were as follows: Reuben, Simeon, Levi, Judah, Issachar, Zebulun, Dan, Naphtali, Gad, Asher, Benjamin, and Joseph (Represented by Ephraim & Manasseh).

We should take notice that the portions of their inherited promised land were not the same. There were many different reasons for this. What I am sure of is that it does not matter how much land you've inherited as much as it matters what you do with the land you have inherited. It is the parable of the talents found in:

Matthew 25:14–30 "It would be like a man going on a journey, who called his servants and entrusted his wealth to them. To one he gave five bags of gold, to another two bags, and to another one bag, each according to his ability. Then he went on his journey. The man who had received five bags of gold went at once and put his money to work and gained five bags more. So also, the one with two bags of gold gained two more. But the man who had received one bag went off, dug a hole in the ground, and hid his master's money. "After a long time the master of those servants returned and settled accounts with them. The man who had received five bags of gold brought the other five. 'Master,' he said, 'you entrusted me with five bags of gold. See, I have gained five more.' "His master replied, 'Well done, good and faithful servant! You have been faithful with a few things; I will put you in charge of many things. Come and share your master's happiness!' "The man with two bags of gold also came. 'Master,' he said, 'you entrusted me with two bags of gold; see, I have gained two more.' "His master replied, 'Well done, good and faithful servant! You have been faithful with a few things; I will put you in charge of many things. Come and share your master's happiness!'

"Then the man who had received one bag of gold came. 'Master,' he said, 'I knew that you are a hard man, harvesting where you have not sown and gathering where you have not scattered seed. So I was afraid and went out and hid your gold in the ground. See, here is what belongs to you.' "His master replied, 'You wicked, lazy servant! So you knew that I harvest where I have not sown and gather where I have not scattered seed? Well then, you should have put my money on deposit with the bankers, so that when I returned I would have received it back with interest. " 'So take the bag of gold from him and give it to the one who has ten bags.

They were dealt with according to what they did with what they had, not how much they had. The lesson to be learned here is that we will all have to give an account for what we did with the inheritance we were given. **We do not have time to be envious of others or be involved in inheritance disputes.**

CHAPTER 10

GOD IS YOUR INHERITANCE

God Is Your Inheritance

According to the Bible, the 12 tribes of Israel received separate portions of land when the Promised Land was divided among them. Each tribe was allocated its own territory; however, the tribe of Levi was not given a specific land but instead received cities and pasture lands within the other tribes' territories to fulfill their priestly duties. According to Deuteronomy 10:9 The Levites were not given land because they were considered to have the Lord as their inheritance.

At the end of the day, it is the Levite blessing that we all desire. Not the stuff but the Savior. Not the material but the magnificent God. Not things but the king of kings. We desire to have God as our inheritance. Outside of the blessing that was bestowed upon the tribe of Judah, which was the lineage of Jesus, the truth of the matter is that the Levites received the best inheritance. What they were given could never be taken away from them by any enemy. God was their inheritance, and God would never leave or forsake them. Their portion was to serve before the Lord all the days of their lives.

The enemy has tried to keep us ignorant of this revelation even to this day. God is our inheritance. For the most part, God's children have lived as if God were against them instead of for them. I have good news, brothers and sisters: God is for us! As Paul writes in Romans 8:31, "What, then, shall we say in response to these things? If God is for us, who can be against us?"

In scripture, God being the Levites' inheritance meant that instead of receiving a portion of land like the other tribes of Israel, the Levites were provided for by the offerings brought to the temple, essentially receiving God's direct provision through their dedicated service as priests, allowing them to focus fully on their religious duties without the concerns of managing land or material wealth; their inheritance was the privilege of serving God directly. This, too, is our inheritance! Remember what Jesus said in Matthew 6:25-34

"Therefore I tell you, do not worry about your life, what you will eat or drink; or about your body, what you will wear. Is not life more than food, and the body more than clothes? Look at the birds of the air; they do not sow or reap or store away in barns, and yet your heavenly Father feeds them. Are you not much more valuable than they? Can any one of you by worrying add a single hour to your life? "And why do you worry about clothes? See how the flowers of the field grow. They do not labor or spin. Yet I tell you that not even Solomon in all his splendor was dressed like one of these. If that is how God clothes the grass of the field, which is here today and tomorrow is thrown into the fire, will he not much more clothe you—you of little faith? So do not worry, saying, 'What shall we eat?' or 'What shall we drink?' or 'What shall we wear?'

God was saying focus on me. I am your inheritance! **When we worry, we show that we lack revelation of our inheritance.**

What It Means for God to Be Your Inheritance

The concept of God as our inheritance is a life-changing truth. It reminds us of the personal relationship, deep connection, provision, and purpose God has for us. When the Scripture declares that God Himself is our inheritance, it is an invitation to explore the richness of His presence and the fullness of life He offers us. It is an invitation to take the wild adventure into your inherited promised land. Here are five truths on what it means for God to be our inheritance.

A Relationship of Intimacy and Belonging

At its core, God as our inheritance means that we belong to Him, and He belongs to us. King Solomon states in Song of Songs 6:3, "I am my beloved's, and my beloved is mine…" This relationship is deeply personal and intimate. In Psalm 73:26, the psalmist declares, "My flesh and my heart may fail, but God is the strength of my heart and my portion forever." This inheritance is not material but relational, signifying that God Himself is the source of our ultimate fulfillment.

When God is our inheritance, we are reminded that His presence is our greatest treasure. This is what he wanted the people of Israel to learn as they went through the wilderness. He was a fire by night and a cloud by day. His presence was with them. It was their inheritance as children of God to have their father walk with them through dark places. It assures us that, no matter what we face in life, we are never alone. This divine intimacy fills the voids of our hearts, offering us love, peace, and joy that surpasses all understanding.

The Promise of Eternal Life

To inherit God is to inherit eternal life with Him. This inheritance is greater than all earthly possessions. In Revelation 21:3-4, we are given a glimpse of this eternal promise: "They will be His people, and God Himself will be with them and be their God. He will wipe every tear from their eyes. As the old gospel song written by the famous singer Andre Crouch says, "Soon, and very soon, we are going to see the king, no more crying there, we are going to see the king." Eternal life is not only an unending existence; it is life to its fullest, where we live in the glory of God's presence. This inheritance gives us peace, hope, joy, and assurance, reminding us that our future is secure in Him.

A Source of Strength and Provision

God being our inheritance also means that He is our ultimate source of strength, provision, and sufficiency. In Lamentations 3:24, the prophet Jeremiah declares, "The Lord is my portion; therefore, I will wait for Him." The word "portion" here has two meanings. First, it means: Territory. In other words, God is my territory. God is my inheritance. The second meaning is that God is enough for us. I love it! The revelation is the territory that God has given to me is enough for me. In the same light, the territory that God has given to you is enough for you. My inheritance is enough. Stop eyeing other people's land. What God has given you is enough for you. You don't have to freak out in the storms of life. When everything else fails, God remains faithful, providing for our every need. He is enough for us. We can trust in His provision rather than striving for worldly security. It teaches us to depend on Him, knowing He is faithful to sustain us in every season of life. He is enough for us.

An Identity Rooted in Christ

When God is our inheritance, our identity is no longer tied to earthly status, possessions, or achievements. Instead, our inheritance is rooted in our relationship with Him. 1 Peter 2:9 describes believers as "a chosen people, a royal priesthood, a holy nation, God's special possession." This identity is not something we earn but a gift we receive through His grace. It is part of our inheritance. This inheritance reminds us that we are deeply valued and loved by God. It frees us from the need to seek validation from people or the world, empowering us to live boldly and confidently in our calling. This is our inherited identity.

Living as Heirs of God

Understanding our inheritance from God is about acknowledging what we have received and embracing the responsibility that comes with it. We call this stewardship. As heirs, we are called to reflect His character, share His love with others, and steward the gifts and blessings He has entrusted to us. Galatians 4:7 reminds us, "So you are no longer a slave, but God's child; and since you are His child, God has made you also an heir."

Our inheritance from God as our Father is both a privilege and a calling. It assures us of His love, righteousness, power, and eternal promises while challenging us to live in a way that honors Him. As we walk in this inheritance, we can confidently face life's challenges, knowing that we are deeply loved, empowered, and destined for an eternal future with Him. Ultimately, this is a call to stewardship. We are to be good stewards of the grace that we have inherited.

Flawed & Forgiven

We are flawed. It is part of our inheritance, given to us by the first Adam. Adam failed in a garden, but Jesus was found in a garden before he was crucified, praying for you and me. We are redeemed and forgiven, it is part of our inheritance given to us by the second Adam (Jesus). We were broken, so he allowed himself to be what we were: broken. Through his brokenness, we have become whole. By His stripes, we are healed, not only physically but mentally and spiritually.

CHAPTER 11

THE MARRIAGE PROPOSAL

The Bride of Christ

Maybe up to this point, you have struggled with the idea of being a son or daughter of God to whom he has given an inheritance. God knew that some of us would have bad experiences as children that might make it difficult for us to understand his love for us. So, he gave us multiple parables and perspectives on how much he loves us. One of the perspectives God gave us was that we are the Bride of Christ. Here are just a few examples in God's word when he speaks of us as His Bride.

Revelation 22:17

The Spirit and the bride say, "Come!" And let the one who hears say, "Come!" Let the one who is thirsty come; and let the one who wishes take the free gift of the water of life.

Ephesians 5:25-27

Husbands, love your wives, just as Christ also loved the church and gave Himself for her, that He might sanctify and cleanse her with the washing of water by the word, that He might present her to Himself a glorious church, not having spot or wrinkle or any such thing, but that she should be holy and without blemish.

Revelation 19:7-9

Let us rejoice and be glad and give him glory! For the wedding of the Lamb has come, and his bride has made herself ready. Fine linen, bright and clean, was given her to wear." (Fine linen stands for the righteous acts of God's holy people.) Then the angel said to me, "Write this: Blessed are those who are invited to the wedding supper of the Lamb!" And he added, "These are the true words of God."

2 Corinthians 11:2

For I am jealous for you with godly jealousy. For I have betrothed you to one husband, that I may present you as a chaste virgin to Christ.

Isaiah 54:5

For your Maker is your husband, The LORD of hosts is His name; And your Redeemer is the Holy One of Israel; He is called the God of the whole earth.

If you will not receive your inheritance as a son or daughter, then receive it as a bride. A bride who is loved, adored, and protected by her husband.

God spoke of us in relationship to him, whether it be son, daughter, or wife, because he wanted to make sure that we got the inheritance. As a child of God he says the inheritance is yours because you were born of me. You have my DNA. You are mine. As a wife (Bride), he says I chose you. I betrothed you. Even if you were not born here, I choose you, and you are the love of my life. You are my wife, and according to the legal law, what I have is yours.

God Has No Prenups

God has no prenups. A prenup is defined as an agreement made by a couple before they marry concerning the ownership of their respective assets should the marriage fail. He knows that he can keep his word concerning us. He has decided that all that He has belongs to us. Just the opposite, we come into our relationship with God with a prenup mindset. We often hold something back or hide a little for ourselves just in case this does not work. Then, we blame God when the relationship does not seem to work as we wanted it to. The truth is we never brought our whole hearts to the relationship. God is not withholding anything from us. The inheritance is ours, so let's not withhold our hearts from God.

God does not make us sign a prenup. A prenuptial agreement is a legally binding contract between two individuals entering a marriage that defines how their assets will be divided in the event of a divorce. It is rooted in the concept of protecting individual ownership and establishing clear terms for potential separation.

Prenuptial agreements reflect a mindset of preparing for the possibility of failure in a union that was intended to be lifelong. God does not make us sign a "prenup" because His relationship with us is based on inheritance. It is based on unconditional love and grace, not conditional agreements. When God enters into a covenant with His people, He does so with a full understanding of their flaws and imperfections.

His love is sacrificial and enduring, as seen in Romans 5:8, where it states, "But God demonstrates His own love for us in this: While we were still sinners, Christ died for us." Marriage ultimately becomes a process where two become one. In other words, what's yours is mine, and what's mine is yours. From us, God inherits the bad, but from God, we inherit the good. The absence of a "prenup" in God's covenant with humanity shows the depth of His commitment toward his bride. He does not require us to prove our worthiness or establish conditions for His love and faithfulness. Instead, God demonstrates a love that is irrevocable and unbreakable, even when we fall short.

Transfer on Death (TOD)

A (TOD) or Transfer on Death is a process that allows you to legally transfer your inheritance directly to your loved ones immediately upon your death without the interference of courts. We see this phenomenon happen in scripture.

Matthew 27:50-53

And when Jesus had cried out again in a loud voice, he gave up his spirit. At that moment the curtain of the temple was torn in two from top to bottom. The earth shook, the rocks split and the tombs broke open. The bodies of many holy people who had died were raised to life. They came out of the tombs after Jesus' resurrection and went into the holy city and appeared to many people.

The word of God tells us that the moment Jesus died, he cried out and gave up his spirit, and the curtain of the temple was torn in two from top to bottom. The curtain temple was 60 feet high and 4 inches thick. The very moment Jesus died, it ripped from top to bottom. The sound would have been long and loud. It would have sounded like thunder. It represented the fact that mankind now had access to the holy of holies. Mankind now had access to God. There was an immediate - Transfer on Death (TOD).

It goes on to say that the earth shook, the rocks split, and the tombs broke open. Why? There was an immediate - Transfer on Death (TOD). The spiritual world was literally changing the physical world. Inheritance was being given without interference. The price had been paid, and the decision had been made.

Then there was the grand-finale. The bodies of many holy people who had died were raised to life. They came out of the tombs after Jesus' resurrection, went into the holy city, and appeared to many people. It was a clear physical sign that there was an immediate - Transfer on Death (TOD).

I am reminded of Colossians 3:23-24 which states: Whatever you do, work at it with all your heart, as working for the Lord, not for human masters, **since you know that you will receive an inheritance from the Lord as a reward**. It is the Lord Christ you are serving.

Since you know… Know what? That you have an inheritance. Paul challenged us to live like we have received a Transfer on Death. Whatever you do, live like a Transfer on Death has taken place. Live like you know you have received an inheritance as a reward from the Lord.

CHAPTER 12

INHERITANCE HIJACKING

Inheritance Hijacking

What is inheritance hijacking? Inheritance hijacking, also known as inheritance theft, is when someone steals an inheritance that was intended for someone else. **God left us a beautiful inheritance, and the enemy wants it.** The entire spiritual battle that we see in:

Ephesians 6:12 For our struggle is not against flesh and blood, but against the rulers, against the authorities, against the powers of this dark world, and against the spiritual forces of evil in the heavenly realms.

This entire fight is over our inheritance. Satan's thought was since I can't stop them, I will steal from them. He wants to keep our inheritance hidden from us. You have heard it said that ignorance is bliss. I say, "Ignorance is missed opportunities." **The devil desires to keep us ignorant of our inheritance.**

The Parable of the Tenants

To discover the modus operandi of the enemy of our souls, we turn to the Gospel of Matthew. It is here that the motive of the enemy is exposed.

Matthew 21:33-38 "33 There was a landowner who planted a vineyard. He put a wall around it, dug a winepress in it and built a watchtower. Then, he rented the vineyard to some farmers and moved to another place. 34 When the harvest time approached, he sent his servants to the tenants to collect his fruit. 35 "The tenants seized his servants; they beat one, killed another, and stoned a third. 36 Then he sent other servants to them, more than the first time, and the tenants treated them the same way. 37 Last of all, he sent his son to them. 'They will respect my son,' he said. **38 "But when the tenants saw the son, they said to each other, 'This is the heir. Come, let's kill him and take his inheritance…"**

Let this statement burn within your soul. **This is the heir. Come, let's kill him and take his inheritance.** Every temptation and trial you face in your life, this is the enemies purpose for the attack. This is the heir. Come, let's kill him or her and take their inheritance. He desires your inheritance.

Imposter Syndrome

I find it interesting that in this portion of scripture, they are well aware of one thing, and that was who the heir was. While this is a simple truth (the son), the power behind it is what is known as imposter syndrome. This is when a person feels like a fraud or inadequate, even though they have achieved great success. They battle self-doubt, fear of being exposed as a fraud, negative self-talk, and find themselves avoiding life's challenges because of this mindset.

Isn't it funny that often, it is not the enemy who has a problem confirming who we are as heirs? It's typically us struggling with imposter syndrome, questioning if we are heirs. The enemy knows who we are, heirs of the kingdom; the question is, do we? My friend, we are not imposters by any means. We cannot fake the crucifixion of the savior, it happened. Because it happened we have become sons and daughters. My biological children don't have to fake like they are mine, DNA proves that they are. It is the same with God and His children. You have God's DNA (Devine Nature Activated) in you. We are sons and daughters of inherited grace.

What Satan Fears

Satan fears the inherited truth that is found in Ephesians 1:18-20 I pray that the eyes of your heart may be enlightened in order that you may know the hope to which he has called you, the riches of his glorious inheritance in his holy people and his incomparably great power for us who believe. That power is the same as the mighty strength he exerted when he raised Christ from the dead and seated him at his right hand in the heavenly realms…

The apostle Paul prayed for the believers in Ephesus, and he prayed that the eyes of their hearts be opened to what? First, to the love of God that they might know him, and second, to the inherited truth of who they were in Christ. Paul was saying I pray that your eyes be open to the inheritance that you have in God. Paul goes on to describe how beautiful and powerful our inheritance is. He describes it as the richest of his glorious inheritance. I don't know about you, but I long to experience the richness of the glorious inheritance that God has for me. In addition, he says that it is an incomparably great power. My friend, there is an inherited power inside of us that is hard to comprehend. To be more specific, Paul says, "That power is the same as the mighty strength God exerted when He raised Christ from the dead and seated him at his right hand in the heavenly realms." Now you know what Satan fears. He fears a believer who knows who he or she is and is walking in their inheritance. **Satan fears a son or daughter of God who is not easily moved by life's storms because they understand that by inheritance, they are the storm.**

Leave an Inheritance

God believes in inheritance so much that he sets it as a standard for believers and their children.

Proverbs 13:22

 A good person leaves an inheritance for their children's children, but a sinner's wealth is stored up for the righteous.

A good, godly person leaves an inheritance for the next generation. While I do not exclude finances from this inheritance, we will focus on all aspects of inheritance, as we have this entire book.

I cannot leave an inheritance of prayer for my children if I do not have a prayer life. I cannot leave an inheritance of faith for my children if they watch me live in fear instead of faith. I cannot leave an inheritance of the importance of God's word if they never hear me declare it and stand on it in the midst of a storm.

I need a revelation, an encounter with God that becomes so real in my everyday life that it impacts my children's children. **In other words, they cannot inherit what I have failed to implement.**

Inspiration For Your Inheritance

In the book of Hebrews we find inspiration for our inheritance. Chapter 11 is known as the Hall of Faith. It is a list of believers, sons, and daughters who lived out their inheritance. I believe that God placed the hall of faith in his word to inspire and encourage us as believers. At some point, it should make us ask, "If they can walk in their inheritance, why can't I?" The answer is, "We can!" The hall of faith is full of flawed people who got a revelation and stepped into their inheritance.

Now you know the importance of inheritance. Now you know what Jesus left you, what the enemy has tried to steal from you, and why. **Your Inheritance Awaits You.**

Until you find yourself you will always be someone else. Become yourself, it's your Inheritance

(Myles Munroe)

<u>**Invite Brian To Speak At Your:**</u>

Corporate Meetings
Church's
Colleges
School Assemblies
Sports Teams (College & Professional)
Mens Conferences
Youth Conferences
Power of Dad seminar or conference in your city

For More Information
Brian Pruitt Motivational (BPM)
or
Power of Dad (POD)

Visit Our Web-Sites Located At:
www.pruittmotivational.com
www.powerofdad.org

Brian Pruitt Products

Brian Pruitt Books

Four For The King

The Power of Dad

Forgiving Our Fathers

The13th Disciple

The Father Forty-Day Challenge

Fight Like A Man

Wounded Lions

Curriculum For Fathers & Fatherless Youth

Power of Dad Mentoring Program

Phase 1-3 Facilitator Manuals

Phase 1-3 Participant Workbooks

Contact Brian Pruitt
To Speak At Your Next Event!

If you would like **Brian Pruitt to come an speak at your next event** or provide **certified John Maxwell Team Leadership Training** here's how you can contact us:

Address:
Brian Pruitt
P.O. Box 294
Saginaw, MI 48606

Phone: (989) 714-5213

Web: www.powerofdad.org
www.pruittmotivational.com

Email: www.pruittmotivational@gmail.com